Practical
CHINESE
COOKING

By Chan Kan Min

 JAPAN PUBLICATIONS, INC.

Practical Chinese Cooking

© 1969 by Chan Kan Min

First Printing, 1969

Library of Congress Catalog Card Number 71-80048

Published by

JAPAN PUBLICATIONS, INC., TOKYO

Distributed by

JAPAN PUBLICATIONS TRADING COMPANY

1225 Howard St., San Francisco, Calif. 94103

175 Fifth Ave., New York, N.Y. 10010

PO Box 5030 Tokyo International, Tokyo, Japan

Photographs by Toshihiro Imamura

Illustrations by Kazuko Terashima

Printed in Japan by Toppan Printing Company, Ltd.

FOREWORD

To enhance the dietary practices of peoples everywhere by teaching the historical heritage of Chinese cookery not only exalts the virtues of those who have contributed to the creation of the cuisine, but is also the cherished ambition of everyone devoted to fine Chinese foods. During my eighteen years of operating a Chinese restaurant in Tokyo, I have studied the foods of not only my native Szechwan but of all regions of China and have been able to give gustatory pleasure to tens of thousands of customers. In the spirit of devotion to my task that has guided me through these years, I recently opened an institute of Chinese cooking to offer unstintingly of my own experience and knowledge of the true essence of Chinese foods. After having received a request from the Japan Publications, Inc. to compile a book of recipes for use in Western nations, I resolved to carry out this task no matter what the cost in time and effort.

The work, however, was not easy. First of all, in a book of this kind the more than 5,000 extant recipes must be trimmed to approximately 60, a practical minimum for Western cooks. Furthermore, since these dishes are only the most commonplace, they cannot enable a person to evolve a true estimation or judgement of the finest aspects of the Chinese cuisine. I realize that I have not explained the culinary processes with total accuracy, but since Chinese cooking is highly complicated and subtle, I felt that helping to make my recipes intelligible as an English text was as much my responsibility as the duty of the editor and translator.

Since even the most complete English dictionaries lack words to accurately explain Chinese cooking methods, I doubted my ability to achieve the understanding that I want from my readers in even simple matters; the problem intensifies, of course, when profound philosophical questions and sophisticated culinary techniques enter the picture. Fortunately, however, the people who cooperated with me in the editorial phases of my work, labored diligently, and we have gradually broken through the language barrier. I am certain that, as a result of our endeavors, cooks who undertake to recreate my dishes will be able to correct current mistaken impressions of Chinese food and will gradually learn its true excellence for themselves.

Summer, 1969

Chan Kan Min

CONTENTS ━━━━━━━━━━━━━━━━━━━━

Tempura-style Prawns and Shrimps

Batter-fried Shrimps

INGREDIENTS

    5 oz small peeled, deveined shrimps
    1 egg white
    5 heaping tbsp flour
    A. Seasonings
    (for shrimp)
    dash salt
    dash monosodium glutamate
    dash pepper
    1 tbsp cornstarch
    B. Batter
    2 tbsp cornstarch
    5 heaping tbsp flour
    1 egg white
    7½ tbsp water
    1½ tsp baking powder
    ½ tsp salt
    1 tsp monosodium glutamate
    1½ tbsp oil
    dash black sesame seeds

PREPARATIONS
1. Mix the shrimp with the salt, monosodium glutamate, pepper, and the cornstarch; set aside.
2. Mix all of the ingredients in B with the hands to make a batter.
3. Add the shrimps to the batter, and mix until they are thoroughly coated.

FRYING
Heat oil in a thick-bottomed pan until it is approximately 300 degrees F. (moderate). Fry the coated shrimps one at a time until they are lightly browned. Just before serving, return them to the oil, and fry them briefly at a high heat.   (If you are frying all of the shrimp together, remove the ones put in first early, so that all will be cooked about the same amount of time.) Serve with catchup.

FRYING HINTS
1.   Use plenty of oil.
2.   Maintain a constant oil temperature. Since putting in all the shrimp at once suddenly lowers the temperature, it is best to add them gradually and to take them out of the oil as quickly as possible.
3.   To test the oil temperature, drop a small quantity of batter into it. You may begin frying the shrimp if the batter first sinks to the bottom and then quickly rises to the surface. When the oil is above 355 degrees F., the batter will not sink but will remain dancing about on the surface. Should the oil begin to smoke, it has already reached temperatures as high as from 375 to 395 degrees F. Remember that oil temperature must be adjusted to the type and size of the food. All deep-fat fried foods should be golden brown, fragrant and crisp on the outside, and moist, but thoroughly cooked, on the inside.

Batter-fried Prawns

INGREDIENTS
    4 prawns
    1 oz ham
    2 oz boned chicken breasts
    1 egg (separated)
    Seasonings
    (for prawns)
    dash salt
    dash sake
    dash pepper
    dash monosodium glutamate
    (for chicken breasts)
    1 egg white
    small amounts monosodium glutamate, pepper, salt, and sake

salt to two part pepper.

NOTE: Whereas deep fat frying produces a golden color over the entire prawn, cooked with this method they are slightly charred on the bottom and comparatively white on top.

Batter
1 heaping tbsp cornstarch
3 heaping tbsp flour
4 tbsp water
1 yellow of an egg

PREPARATIONS

1. Peel and devein the prawns, leaving the tail shell on. Wash them, and dry them carefully with a towel. Open them, and make small slits in the sides (see illus.) so that they will not curl up when fried.
2. Sprinkle salt, monosodium glutamate, sake, and pepper on the prawns.
3. Finely crush the chicken breasts with a knife. Mix them with the white of an egg, sake, monosodium glutamate, pepper, and salt. Dilute the mixture with 5 tbsp water, and let stand.
4. Mix the cornstarch, flour, water, and yellow of an egg into a batter.
5. Dip the prawns in cornstarch; place a small amount of the chicken mixture on each, and sprinkle chopped ham on top. Place the covered prawns in a steamer, and steam for six or seven minutes.

FRYING

1. Coat the bottoms of the steamed prawns with batter. Heat a thick bottom skillet and spread a small amount of oil over the bottom. Arrange the prawns one by one in the skillet. Next add one ladle of oil, and continue cooking, pouring the heated oil over the tops of the prawns.
2. When the oil reaches a high temperature, add more cold oil. Repeat the process until the prawns are thoroughly cooked.
3. Arrange on a platter and serve with side dishes of catchup and a mixture of one part

Minced Shrimp and Pork in Bean-curd Skin Rolls

INGREDIENTS

4 oz shrimp
4 oz ground pork
6 arrowhead bulbs (approximately 2 oz)
1 oz green peas
2 sheets bean-curd skin
1 egg
Seasonings
(for filling)
¼ tsp salt
1 tbsp sake
dash pepper
½ tsp monosodium glutamate
2 tbsp cornstarch
1 egg white
Batter
1 egg yolk
2 tbsp water
2 heaping tbsp flour
1 tbsp cornstarch
small amounts sesame seed oil, catchup, and cornstarch

PREPARATIONS

1. Mince the shrimp.
2. Crush the arrowhead roots.
3. Cut the bean-curd skin sheets in half.

SEASONING

1. Mix the ground pork, minced shrimp, arrowhead roots, and green peas well. Add an egg white, salt, sake, pepper, and monosodium glutamate. Mix until the ingredients cohere. Next add two tbsp of cornstarch, and mix again.

2. In a separate bowl, make a thin batter with the yellow of an egg, water, flour, and cornstarch.

PREPARING THE ROLLS

1. Divide the pork and shrimp mixture into four equal parts, place some on each of the four sheets of bean-curd skin, and roll as shown in the illustration. Bind the rolls together by spreading a thin coat of batter on the inside to serve as an adhesive. Fold the ends inward.

2. Oil a plate, put the rolls on it, and steam them for five or six minutes. Cut one to determine whether the inside is done; if it is not, steam longer.

FRYING

Heat about one and one-half inches of oil in a deep frying pan. Dip the rolls in cornstarch, and lightly coat them with batter.

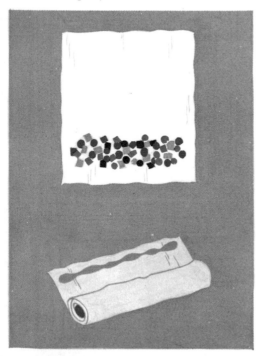

Put them one by one in the hot oil, and fry till thoroughly heated and golden brown. Remove from oil and drain well. Cut each roll into bite-size pieces, arrange on a platter, and coat them lightly with sesame seed oil. Serve with a side dish of catchup.

Minced bamboo shoots, Japanese forest mushrooms, or champignons may be used in place of the arrowhead roots.

FRYING HINTS

1. If you fry the rolls while they are still hot from steaming, use a high heat, and fry quickly until the batter coating is golden brown.

2. If the rolls have cooled before you begin frying, use a moderate heat until the batter is set; then raise it for the final crisping. In this case be especially careful to drain the oil from them thoroughly before serving.

3. When in a rush, you may fry the rolls without steaming, but the results are less satisfactory. Prepare the rolls ahead of time, and you can fry them quickly whenever they are needed.

Prawns and Onions in Sweet and Sour Sauce (See page 38.)

INGREDIENTS

3 prawns
½ onion
Seasonings
(for prawns)
dash pepper
dash sake
dash salt
dash monosodium glutamate
2 tbsp flour
Sauce
1 tbsp sake
3 tbsp vinegar
3 tbsp soy sauce
3 tbsp sugar
1 tbsp catchup
1½ tbsp cornstarch and water mixture

PREPARATIONS

1. Remove prawn heads, but leave the shells on. Cut each into three sections.

2. Peel the onion, and cut it vertically (see

illus.).

1. Sprinkle the pepper, sake, salt, and monosodium glutamate on the prawns, and roll them in flour.

COOKING

1. Heat about one and one-half inches of oil in a thick-bottom pan to about 300 degrees F. Carefully fry the prawns one by one.

2. Add the onions, and cook until they are well coated with oil. Remove both onions and prawns.

3. Pour off most of the oil, and add the sake, vinegar, soy sauce, sugar, and catchup to the pan. Mix well and bring to a boil. Return the prawns and onions to the pan, and thicken the mixture with a blend of cornstarch and water.

Prawns and Potato Chips with Sweet and Sour Sauce

INGREDIENTS
    4 prawns
    3 potatoes
    Seasonings
    (for prawns)
    ⅛ tsp salt

dash monosodium glutamate
1 tsp sake
½ egg white
1½ tbsp cornstarch
Sauce
3 tbsp soy sauce
1 tbsp vinegar
1 heaping tbsp sugar
3 tbsp water
dash monosodium glutamate
1 tbsp cornstarch and water mixture

PREPARATIONS

1. Peal, clean, and devein the prawns; cut each into three or four sections.

2. Peel the potatoes, and cut them into thin rectangular slices (see illus.).

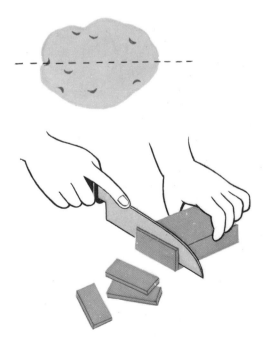

3. Put the prawn sections in a bowl together with the salt, monosodium glutamate, sake, egg white, and cornstarch.

4. Soak the potatoes in water for a few minutes. Remove them, dry them well with a cloth, and deep fry in hot oil (320 degree F.) until they are golden brown. Heap them on a plate to drain.

COOKING

1. Lower the heat, add the prawn sections one by one, and fry them for only about thirty seconds, or until they turn white. Pile them on top of the potato chips.

2. Heat one tbsp of oil in another pan. Add the sauce ingredients. When the mixture boils, thicken it with the cornstarch mixture.

Pour the sauce over the prawns and potatoes, and serve immediately.

Shrimp, Tomatoes, and Onions with Catchup Sauce

INGREDIENTS

  6 oz small shrimp
  1 tomato
  1 onion
  1 oz green peas
  Seasonings
  dash salt
  1 tsp sake
  dash monosodium glutamate
  dash pepper
  1 tbsp cornstarch
  ½ egg white
  Sauce
  ⅓ tsp salt
  1 tbsp sake
  1 tbsp sugar
  ⅓ tsp monosodium glutamate
  1 tbsp cornstarch and water mixture
  3 tbsp soup stock
  1 tbsp catchup

PREPARATIONS

1. Finely dice tomato and onion.

2. Let the cleaned shrimp stand for a few minutes in the salt, sake, monosodium glutamate, pepper, cornstarch, and egg white.

3. Mix all of the sauce ingredients in a separate bowl.

COOKING

1. Heat an empty pan; pour in one or two cups of oil and swish it about until the bottom and sides are thoroughly coated. Return the oil to its original container. Pour in three cups of fresh oil, and heat to from 250 to 280 degrees F. Put the shrimps into the pan, and stirring them gently, coat them well with oil. Remove and drain.

2. Sauté the tomato in the catchup. Add all the other ingredients, bring to a boil, thicken with cornstarch mixture, and serve.

Piquant Szechwan Shrimp

INGREDIENTS

  6 oz shelled shrimp
  2 oz green peas
  Seasonings
  (for shrimp)
  ¼ tsp salt
  ¼ tsp monosodium glutamate
  dash pepper
  1 tbsp cornstarch
  ½ egg white
  1 tbsp oil
  Sauce
  small piece of fresh ginger root
  ½ leek
  ½ clove garlic
  ½ tsp chopped red pepper
  2 tbsp catchup
  2 tbsp oil
  ⅓ tsp salt
  dash monosodium glutamate
  1 tbsp sake
  2 tbsp sugar
  ½ tsp vinegar
  1 tbsp cornstarch and water mixture
  3 tbsp soup stock

PREPARATIONS

1. Let the shrimp stand in the seasonings for a few minutes.

2. Chop the ginger and garlic. Chop the onion separately, and put it in a separate container.

COOKING

1. Heat the pan, pour in one cup of oil; swish it about to cover the sides and bottom. Return the oil to its container.

2. Pour in three cups of fresh oil, and heat to a moderate temperature. Dip the shrimp into the oil one by one. Remove and drain.

3. Into the same pan, pour two tbsp of oil, and sauté the ginger, garlic, chopped red pepper, and catchup over a high heat. Add the soup stock. Remove the pan from the heat. Add salt, monosodium glutamate, wine, and sugar. Taste and correct if necessary. Add the shrimp, green peas, and chopped onion; mix quickly. Thicken with cornstarch mixture, sprinkle in vinegar, and stirring constantly, add the oil. Serve hot.

This spicy dish, whose deep, golden color, thick sauce, well blended flavors, and sweet-sour tang are famous all over China, uses a number of seasonings; consequently, care is required in both measuring and adding them to the other ingredients.

Fried Toast with Quail Eggs

INGREDIENTS

    2 oz small shelled shrimp
    3 oz boned chicken breast
    2 oz pork fat
    2 arrowhead root
    6 quail eggs
    Seasonings

    dash salt
    dash pepper
    dash monosodium glutamate
    1 tbsp sake
    1½ tbsp cornstarch
    3 tbsp water

PREPARATIONS

Fine chop together the shrimp, chicken breast, and pork fat. (First pound with the back of a knife, and then chop.)

2. Chop the arrowhead root fine.

3. Add 1 egg white, salt, pepper, monosodium glutamate, and sake to the chopped ingredients. Mix well, taste, season further if necessary, and add the cornstarch.

4. Hard boil the quail eggs.

STEAMING

Spread the chopped ingredients on bread from which the crust has been removed. Cut the boiled eggs in half, and press them into the spread. Sprinkle the top of the egg with cornstarch, white sesame seeds, and chopped parsely. Steam for four or five minutes. The sandwiches will fry better, if you allow them to cool after steaming.

FRYING

Deep fat fry the toast, cut each slice into quarters, and serve.

FRYING HINTS

If the bread has chilled, fry it first at a moderate heat until golden brown; then turn the heat up for the final crisping. Turn the bread from time to time. Drain well on paper.

Walnuts may be used in place of quail eggs; other decorative garnishes include diced ham or chopped peanuts.

Pork Dishes

Fried Pork Balls

INGREDIENTS

9 oz ground pork
6 arrowhead roots
Seasonings
1 egg
¼ tsp salt
1 tbsp water
½ tsp soy sauce
1 tbsp sake
dash pepper
¼ tsp monosodium glutamate
1 tbsp cornstarch
1 tbsp sesame oil

PREPARATIONS

After pounding the arrowhead roots, mix them with the ground pork. Add the egg, salt, water, soy sauce, sake, pepper, and monosodium glutamate. Mix well, until the ingredients cohere. Finally add the cornstarch and sesame oil, and mix again.

FRYING

Heat about one and one-half inches of oil in a deep pan to a moderate temperature (about 285 degrees F.). Form the meat mixture into balls. Taking each ball in a wet spoon, drop gently into the hot oil (see illus.).
If forming the meat by hand is difficult, drop it by spoonfuls into the oil; but the resulting shapes are less pleasing. Fry until the balls are brown; remove and drain.
NOTE: The oil must be only moderately hot. If too hot, the outside of the ball will burn, while the inside remains raw. On the other hand, if the temperature is too low, the balls will crumble.

Sweet and Sour Pork

INGREDIENTS

5 oz lean pork
3½ oz onion
2 green peppers
2 oz dried mushrooms
Seasonings
(for pork and vegetables)
¼ tsp salt
dash sake
dash pepper
dash monosodium glutamate
1 tbsp cornstarch
Batter
½ egg
4 tbsp water
4 heaping tbsp flour
2 heaping tbsp cornstarch

Sauce

1 tbsp soy sauce
2 tbsp vinegar
2 tbsp sugar
1 tbsp sake
¼ tsp salt
½ tsp monosodium glutamate
2 tbsp soup stock
3 tbsp catchup
1½ tbsp cornstarch and water mixture

PREPARATIONS

1. Score the pork lightly, and cut it into one-inch cubes.
2. Cut the onion and green peppers into similar sizes, and diagonally slice mushrooms that have been soaked in warm water for a few minutes.
3. Let the meat stand for a while in a mixture of salt, sake, pepper, monosodium glutamate, and cornstarch.
4. Prepare batter by mixing the egg, water, flour, and cornstarch.
5. Dip the meat in the batter.
6. Mix all the sauce ingredients in a separate bowl.

FRYING

1. Heat and oil a deep pan. Pour in two cups of fresh oil, heat it thoroughly, and fry the meat. When the meat is done and its batter coating golden brown, add the onions, green peppers, and mushrooms. Fry them briefly; then remove and drain.
2. Add two tbsp of oil to the same pan, and pour in the sauce mixture. Stir constantly until the sauce boil and thickens, add one more tbsp of oil, and finally the meat and vegetables.

Pineapple and cherries may be added for brighter color.

Pork and Bean-curd Patties in Sauce (See page 27.)

INGREDIENTS

7 oz ground pork
1 oz Jew's-ear
2½ oz bamboo shoots
½ bean-curd cake
½ egg
small amount spinach

Seasonings
(for meat and bean curd)
¼ tsp salt
3 drops soy sauce
1 tbsp sake
dash pepper
¼ tsp monosodium glutamate
1 heaping tbsp cornstarch

Sauce
3 tbsp soy sauce
1 tbsp sake
dash monosodium glutamate
1 tsp sugar
dash pepper
3 tbsp cornstarch and water mixture
2½ cups soup stock

PREPARATIONS

1. Mix the pork and bean curd in a bowl. Add egg, monosodium glutamate, salt, soy sauce, sake, pepper, and cornstarch. Mix well.
2. Wash all grit from the Jew's-ear, cut the bamboo shoots in thin slices, and clean and cut the spinach in suitable sizes.

COOKING

1. Heat oil in a thick pan to approximately 325 degrees F. and after forming the bean curd and pork mix into three equal patties, fry them till golden brown.
2. Remove the patties to a separate bowl. Pour 1½ cups soup stock, soy sauce, and a dash of pepper into the pan, and simmer for 20 minutes.
3. Add the Jew's-ear, bamboo shoots, meat patties, and spinach, plus soy sauce, sake, monosodium glutamate, sugar, pepper, cornstarch mixture, and remaining soup stock. Simmer until the sauce thickens.

CHINESE RESTAURANT SHISEN HANTEN

CHINESE RESTAURANT SHISEN HANTEN

中華四川料理　六本木　渋谷　四川飯店

Ground Pork and Chinese Vermicelli

INGREDIENTS
4 oz ground pork
9 oz Chinese vermicelli
½ leek
about 1 oz forest mushrooms
Seasonings
2½ tbsp soy sauce
1 tsp sweetened bean paste
1 tbsp sake
1 tsp monosodium glutamate
dash pepper
2 cups soup stock
small amount oil

PREPARATIONS AND COOKING
1. Soften the vermicelli in warm water, and cut it into six-inch lengths.
2. Dice the forest mushrooms.
3. After lightly sautéeing the pork in a small quantity of oil, add sweetened bean paste, soy sauce, sake, monosodium glutamate, and soup stock. Finally add the vermicelli and the diced mushrooms. Simmer.
4. When the soup has almost entirely evaporated, add the chopped leek, and pour one tbsp of oil around the inner edge of the pan. At serving time, a small amount of the soup stock should remain. For added piquance, sprinkle a little red pepper on the vermicelli and meat.
NOTE: The following are the ingredients and proportions for preparing sweetened bean paste.
    11 oz dark or light bean paste
    1½ cups water

5 oz sugar
2 tbsp soy sauce
4 tsp sake
1 tsp monosodium glutamate
5 tbsp salad oil

Steamed Pork with Spinach

INGREDIENTS
11 oz lean pork
small amount spinach
Seasonings
(for meat)
small amounts each of the following
soy sauce
sake
monosodium glutamate
chopped leek
grated ginger root
(for the sauce)
½ cup prepared sauce (see below)
1 cup water
1½ tbsp soy sauce
1 tbsp sugar

PREPARATIONS AND COOKING
1. Simmer the uncut pork in the prepared sauce for about twenty minutes. Remove it.
2. Cut the meat into about six or eight slices. Put it into a bowl containing 1½ tbsp soy sauce, 1 tbsp sugar, 1 tbsp sake, a dash of monosodium glutamate, and the grated ginger root and chopped leek. Put it into the steamer, and steam for from one and one-half to two hours.
3. Heat a small amount of oil in a pan and sauté the spinach. Season with salt, sake, and monosodium glutamate, and heap on a plate. Put the sliced pork and its sauce into the pan, season to taste, add a tbsp of corn-

starch mixed with water to thicken the sauce and a small amount of oil to give gloss. Serve the meat on top of the spinach.

THE SAUCE

Heat ⅔ cup of sugar with ⅓ cup vegetable oil in a pan until the mixture becomes the color of caramel. Add 4 cups of water, and mix well. To this add 1½ tbsp salt, 2 cups soy sauce, 2 cups sugar, ½ cup sake, and a dash of monosodium glutamate. Put the following ingredients in a cheeze-cloth bag, and cook with the meat for greater flavor variety.

15 fennel seeds
30 grains of Japanese pepper
1 oz cinnamon
2 or 3 pieces tangerine skin

Thinly Sliced Pork with Eggs

INGREDIENTS

3 oz pork loin
3 eggs
2 oz bamboo shoots
2 oz Jew's-ear
small amount spinach
½ leek
small amount ginger root
Seasonings
(for meat)
½ egg
dash salt
dash sake
dash baking powder
dash monosodium glutamate
dash pepper
1 tbsp cornstarch
Sauce
1½ tbsp soy sauce
1 tbsp sake
1 tsp vinegar
1 tsp sugar
¼ tsp monosodium glutamate
1 tbsp cornstarch and water mixture
2 tbsp soup or water

PREPARATIONS

1. Slice the pork thin.
2. Slice the bamboo shoots thin, clean them thoroughly, and drain.
3. Cut the leek into one-half-inch lengths and the ginger into thin squares, one-half-inch to a side.
4. Wash the spinach thoroughly, and cut into bite-size pieces.
5. Marinate the meat in the egg, salt, sake, baking powder, monosodium glutamate, pepper, and cornstarch.
6. Break the eggs into a separate bowl, lightly season with salt and monosodium glutamate, and beat well.
7. Mix the sauce ingredients in a separate bowl.

COOKING

1. Heat a pan and coat it with oil; return the oil to its container. Next pour two cups of fresh oil into the pan, heat it, and sauté the marinated meat and the bamboo shoots until they are well coated. Remove and drain.
2. Coat a separate pan with about three tbsp of oil, and fry the eggs until they are light and fluffy. Put them on top of the meat and bamboo shoots. In a small quantity of oil, lightly sauté the leek and ginger, add all the other ingredients, and pour the sauce mixture over them. Stirring contantly and turning the pan to prevent sticking, cook until the sauce thickens. For a spicier version add a dash of red pepper bean paste when you sauté the ginger.

Thinly Sliced Pork Sauté

INGREDIENTS
    6 oz pork loin
    4 oz stalk celery
    8 arrowhead bulbs
    2 oz Jew's-ear (or forest mushrooms or champignons)
    ½ leek
    small amount ginger root
    small amount spinach
    1 garlic clove

Seasonings
(for the meat)
    ¼ tsp salt
    1 tbsp sake
    dash pepper
    ½ tsp monosodium glutamate
    ½ egg
    1 heaping tbsp cornstarch
    1 tbsp oil

Sauce
    1 tbsp soy sauce
    1 tbsp sake
    ⅔ tbsp vinegar
    ⅔ tsp monosodium glutamate
    1 tbsp cornstarch and water mixture
    1½ tbsp soup stock or water
    ⅓ tsp red pepper bean paste
    2 tsp sugar

PREPARATIONS
1. Cut the pork into thin slices and then into one-and-one-half-inch squares.
2. Cut the celery into thin pieces slightly smaller than the pork.
3. Thinly slice the arrowhead bulbs.
4. Soften the Jew's-ear in hot water, remove the stalk, wash out all of the grit.
5. Cut the spinach into bite-size pieces.
6. Dice the leek, ginger, and garlic.
7. Marinate the pork in the salt, sake, pepper, monosodium glutamate, egg, cornstarch, and oil.

COOKING
1. Fry the meat in moderately hot oil until it begins to change color.
2. Lightly fry all of the other ingredients, except the Jew's-ear and the spinach, in the same way. Drain.
3. Oil the bottom and sides of a separate pan.

4. Pour one tbsp of oil into the pan, and after adding one tsp of red pepper bean paste sauté all of the ingredients except the Jew's-ear and spinach. Finally add these last two, pour the sauce ingredients over them, and simmer till the sauce thickens.

Szechwan-style Twice-cooked Pork and Cabbage

INGREDIENTS
    6 oz pork loin
    5 oz cabbage
    1 leek
    1 garlic clove
    pressed bean curd (if available)

Seasonings
    ¼ tsp red pepper bean paste
    1 tbsp sweetened bean paste
    ½ tbsp soy sauce
    1 tbsp sake
    ½ tsp monosodium glutamate

PREPARATIONS
1. Boil the uncut pork for twenty minutes, or until blood does not ooze out when the meat is pierced with a fork.
2. Chill the pork in cold water. Cut into thin slices.
3. Peel off the cabbage leaves one at a time, and remove all hard parts. Cut into large pieces.

COOKING
1. Heat three or four cups of oil in a pan, and quickly fry the cabbage, leek, and pressed bean curd. Remove and drain.

2. Pour off all but two tbsp of oil. Fry the pork on both sides till it changes color. Lightly sauté the sweetened bean paste and the red pepper bean paste. Add the leek and garlic and 1½ tbsp of soy sauce. Mix well. To this add the pressed bean curd and cabbage and one tbsp of sake, and sauté over a high heat, stirring constantly. Sprinkle on the monosodium glutamate, and finally, stirring well, add one tbsp oil to produce a pleasing gloss.

Celery and Shredded Pork

INGREDIENTS

6 oz pork loin
4 oz celery
1 medium carrot
½ leek
small amount ginger root

Seasonings

(for meat)

¼ tsp salt
1 tbsp sake
½ tsp monosodium glutamate
dash pepper
dash baking powder
1 small egg
½ tsp soy sauce
1 tbsp cornstarch
½ tsp oil

Sauce

1 tbsp soy sauce
1 tbsp sake
1 tsp sugar
1 tsp vinegar
½ tsp monosodium glutamate
1 tbsp cornstarch and water mixture
3 tbsp soup stock or water
¼ tsp red pepper bean paste

PREPARATIONS

1. Julienne cut the pork, carrot, celery, and leek. Cut the ginger fine.
2. Into a bowl with the julienne cut pork put the salt, sake, monosodium glutamate, pepper, baking powder, egg, and soy sauce; mix well.

After adding the cornstarch, mix again thoroughly; and finally add the oil.

3. Combine all the sauce ingredients in a small bowl.
4. After oiling the bottom and sides of a heated pan, add three cups of fresh oil. Add the pork and carrot before the oil is hot, and when it begins to bubble, add the celery. Stir constantly. Fry lightly, remove, and drain.
5. Pour one tbsp of oil into another pan, and sauté the ginger and red pepper bean paste. After adding the leek, pork, carrot, and celery, sauté again briefly, and pour on the sauce ingredients. Stir constantly until the sauce thickens. Finally add one tbsp oil for gloss.

Pork Sauté with Chestnuts

INGREDIENTS

6 oz pork loin
2 oz chestnuts
4 oz green peppers
½ leek
small amount of ginger root
½ egg white

Seasonings

(for meat)

¼ tsp salt
2 drops soy sauce
1 tbsp sake
¼ tsp monosodium glutamate
½ egg

dash pepper
dash baking powder
1½ tbsp cornstarch
1 tbsp oil

Sauce

1½ tbsp soy sauce
1 tbsp sake
1½ tsp vinegar
1 tsp sugar
½ tsp monosodium glutamate
1½ tsp cornstarch and water mixture
3 tbsp soup stock

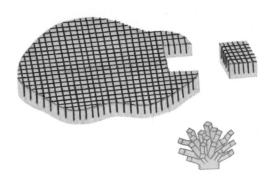

PREPARATIONS

1. Cut the pork into slices about ½ inch thick, and criss-cross cut the top as shown in the illustration. This makes the meat cook faster. Next cut it into squares about ½ of an inch to a side.

2. Wash and seed the green peppers; cut them into ½-inch squares.

3. Cut the leek into ½-inch lengths, peel and slice the ginger root thin.

4. Into a bowl with the cut meat pour the salt, soy sauce, sake, monosodium glutamate, egg, pepper, and baking powder. Mix well. Finally add the cornstarch and the oil, which both seals in flavors and helps the meat open into flower-like shapes.

5. Mix all of the sauce ingredients together in a small bowl.

6. Heat the pan before oiling its sides and bottom. Drain; next add three cups of fresh oil. Fry the meat and green peppers. Remove and drain.

7. Sauté the leeks and ginger lightly in a small amount of oil; add all the other ingredients, and stir quickly until the sauce thickens.

Chicken Dishes

Chicken Wings with Mushrooms and Bamboo Shoots (See page 27.)

INGREDIENTS
    11 oz chicken wings
    4 oz bamboo shoots
    3 oz forest mushrooms
    1 leek
    Seasonings
    2½ tbsp soy sauce
    1 tbsp sake
    ½ tsp sugar
    1 tsp monosodium glutamate
    dash pepper
    2 tbsp cornstarch and water mixture
    3 cups soup stock

PREPARATIONS
·1. Cut off and discard the tips of the wings. Trim away excess skin to make a pleasing shape.

2. Cut the bamboo shoots into comb-like shapes (see illus.); they should be slightly smaller than the chicken wings.

3. Clip the edges of the forest mushrooms in feather form.

4. Cut the leek into three-inch lengths, and split them in half lengthwise if they are thick.

5. To give the wings a bright golden color when fried, let them stand for a while in a mixture of small amounts of sake and soy sauce.

COOKING
1. Into a hot pan pour three cups of oil. Heat it to approximately 360 degrees F., and deep fry the chicken wings.

2. In a small amount of oil in another pan sauté the bamboo shoots, mushrooms, and leek.

Add three cups of soup stock, monosodium glutamate, soy sauce, sake, and pepper. Add the chicken wings, cover, and cook for fifteen minutes over a moderate heat. Finally thicken with the cornstarch and water mixture. Before serving, add one tbsp of oil for gloss.

Devised in a famous Shanghai restaurant about forty years ago, this recipe is a combination of Canton and Szechwan styles. The chicken should be a golden color, its meat should fall easily from the bone when eaten, and the sauce should be fragrant and richly flavored.

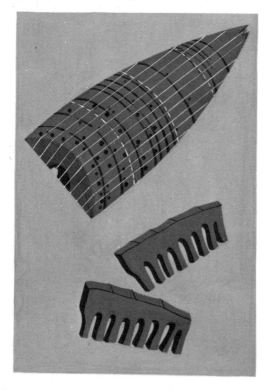

Fried Chicken and Lemon

INGREDIENTS
    ½ frying chicken
    2 slices lemon
    Seasonings
    (for chicken)
    ½ tsp salt
    1 tbsp soy sauce
    Sauce
    ½ tsp salt
    2 tbsp soy sauce
    1½ tbsp sugar
    1 tbsp sake
    ½ tsp monosodium glutamate
    2 tbsp cornstarch and water mixture
    2 tbsp oil
    2½ cups soup stock

PREPARATIONS
1. Rub the inside and outside of the chicken thoroughly with salt, soy sauce, and oil. Let it stand for a while.

2. Cut two slices of lemon.

COOKING

1.   Heat three cups of oil to 355 degree F., and fry the chicken for about five seconds.

2.   Bring 2½ cups of soup stock to a boil in a separate pan.   Add the chicken, lemon, soy sauce, salt, and sugar.   Cover and cook over a low heat for from fifteen to twenty minutes .

3.   Remove the chicken, cut it into convenient pieces, and arrange it pleasingly on a platter.

4.   To the soup, add the cornstarch and water mixture and two tbsp of oil.   Cook until thick.   Pour over the chicken, and serve.

Apple-shape Fried Chicken

INGREDIENTS

6 frying chicken wings
1 oz pine nuts (if unavailable, use chestnuts or peanuts)

Batter
4 heaping tbsp flour
1 egg white
4 tbsp water
dash salt
dash monosodium glutamate
dash baking powder

Seasonings
dash salt
dash monosodium glutamate
dash sake
dash pepper

PREPARATIONS

1. . Cut off and discard the tips of the wings. Sever at the first joint, and peel skin and flesh back to form a ball at one end of the bone (see illus.).   Six wings will produce

twelve such apple shapes.

2.   Dice the pine nuts.

3.   Marinate the prepared chicken in the salt, sake, pepper, and monosodium glutamate.

4.   Prepare a batter from the listed ingredients, and add the diced pine nuts.

COOKING

1.   Heat five cups of oil to about 355 degrees F.   Coat the chicken in batter, and fry each piece, one at a time, until golden brown, and thoroughly done to the bone.   Be careful to preserve the round shape of the chicken when dipping it in batter, and after frying should any strange projections have formed, carefully cut them away.

2.   Serve with sliced tomatoes (see illus.)

CUTTING THE WINGS INTO APPLE SHAPE

Discard the tips.   Fold the ends under. Remove and discard the smaller bone.

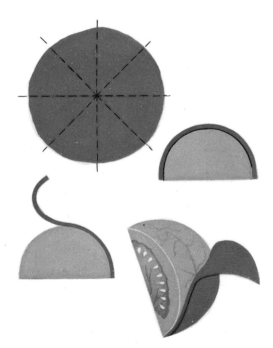

Fried Chicken in Savory Sauce

INGREDIENTS
14 oz frying chicken, cleaned and cut into small
  pieces with bone remaining.
1 leek
1 small piece ginger root
Sauce
3 tbsp soy sauce
2 tbsp vinegar
3 tbsp sugar
small amount sesame seeds

PREPARATIONS
1. Lacerate the thick parts of the chicken meat, and rub in thoroughly a mixture of salt, soy sauce, pepper, and sake. Coat the skin with soy sauce.
2. Dice the leek and the ginger. You should have about three tbsp of leek and about 1 heaping tbsp of ginger.
3. Mix the sauce ingredients in a small bowl, and add the leek and ginger.

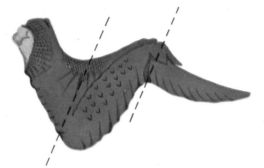

COOKING
1. Fry the chicken in three cups of oil (about 355 degrees F.) at medium heat, for about twenty minutes. Turn from time to time to insure even cooking.
2. When the chicken is golden brown, remove it, and cut it into convenient pieces. Arrange on a plate, and pour the savory sauce over it. The dish will be more attractive if you put the bone sections on the bottom and the fried meat up. Be sure to pour on the sauce while the chicken is hot, because its flavors do not penetrate cold foods well.

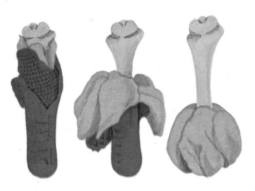

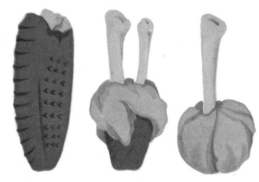

Chicken in Szechwan Sauce
(See page 38.)

INGREDIENTS
½ frying chicken
1 small clove garlic
small amount ginger root
1 leek

Sauce

4 tbsp soy sauce
2 tsp vinegar
1 tbsp sugar
4 tbsp ground sesame seeds
1 tbsp pepper oil (see below)
1 tsp red pepper bean paste
1 tsp monosodium glutamate
1 tbsp sesame seed oil

PREPARATIONS
1. Boil the chicken for about twenty minutes. Let it cool in the stock; then remove it, cut it into convenient pieces, and arrange it on a platter.
2. Dice the garlic and ginger.

COOKING THE SAUCE
The flavors in this sauce must produce a distinctive blend in which no one ingredient predominates.

To prepare pepper oil, cook red pepper in salad oil until the mixture turns black.
1. Blend all the sauce ingredients in a large bowl; and the diced garlic and ginger. Blend thoroughly.
2. Pour the sauce over the boiled chicken, and serve.

Chicken Fried in Cornstarch

INGREDIENTS
14 oz frying chicken cut into pieces with bones
Seasonings

½ tsp soy sauce
¾ tsp salt
½ tsp monosodium glutamate
1 tbsp sake
dash pepper
1 heaping tbsp cornstarch

PREPARATIONS
1. Marinate the chicken pieces in the soy sauce, salt, monosodium glutamate, sake, and

pepper. Add the cornstarch, and coat the chicken well.

COOKING
1. Fry the chicken in four to six cups of oil heated to 320 degrees F.
2. Remove the chicken from time to time and tap it lightly with a spoon or ladle to loosen the meat from the bone and to promote deep cooking. Repeating this process several times, gradually raise the heat to about 340 degrees F. (Unless the heat is increased, the surface of the chicken will harden while the meat remains only partly cooked.)
3. Drain the chicken, and arrange it on a platter. Serve with catchup and a mixture of Japanese pepper and parched salt (proportions 3:7). The latter may be omitted, but it is a fine complement to deep-fat fried foods.

Chicken Breasts with Cucumbers and Mushrooms

INGREDIENTS
6 oz boned chicken breasts
1 cucumber
1 oz forest mushrooms
½ leek
small amount ginger root
2 oz bamboo shoots

Seasonings
(for the chicken)
¼ tsp salt
1 tbsp sake
1 tbsp water
¼ tsp monosodium glutamate
dash baking powder
dash pepper

pepper and egg white. Mix well, and then add the cornstarch and oil. Mix again.

4. Blend all the sauce ingredients in a separate bowl.

1 egg white
1½ tbsp cornstarch
1 tbsp oil

Sauce

¼ tsp salt
1 tsp sugar
1 tbsp sake
½ tsp monosodium glutamate
1 tbsp cornstarch and water mixture
3 tbsp water or soup stock

PREPARATIONS

1. Slice the chicken breasts, bamboo shoots, cucumber, and forest mushrooms thin.

2. Cut the leek into ½-inch lengths, and cut the ginger in thin squares ½ inch to a side.

3. Put the sliced chicken breasts in a bowl with the salt, sake, and water, and allow the meat to absorb all the moisture. Add the monosodium glutamate, baking powder,

COOKING

Use more oil and a smaller pan than is customary for sautéed dishes.

1. Oil the bottoms and sides of a heated pan; return the oil to its container. Pour in three cups of fresh oil, and while it is heating, add the bamboo shoots, mushrooms, and other vegetables. When the oil is hot, add the chicken one piece at a time, and fry it till it is golden brown. Remove all ingredients and drain.

2. To the small amount of oil remaining in the pan, add one additional tbsp. Sauté the ginger and leek. Add the cooked vegetables and chicken and all of the sauce ingredients. Stirring constantly, cook until the sauce thickens. Add one tbsp of oil to prevent rapid cooling and to produce a pleasing gloss. The oil should be poured in from the sides (see illus.), and the food must not be mixed again.

Cutting the cucumber and bamboo shoots in flower shapes enhances the appearance of the dish. Substitute Jew's-ear, mushrooms, or champignons for any of the vegetables that are unobtainable.

Cubed Chicken Sautéed with Mustard

INGREDIENTS
6 oz chicken thighs
1 cucumber
3 green peppers
½ leek
small amount ginger root

Seasonings
(for chicken)
¼ tsp salt
1 tbsp sake
dash pepper
¼ tsp monosodium glutamate
dash baking powder
1 egg
1½ tbsp cornstarch
1 tbsp oil

Sauce
1 tbsp soy sauce
1 tbsp sake
1 tsp vinegar
1 tsp sugar
½ tsp monosodium glutamate
1 tbsp cornstarch and water mixture
2 tbsp soup stock
1 tbsp red pepper bean paste

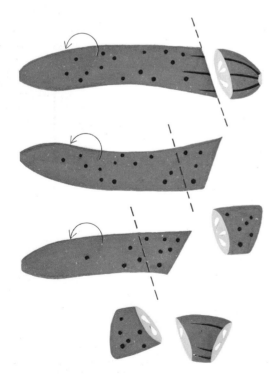

PREPARATIONS
1. Remove the tendons from the meat, and cut it into 1-inch cubes.
2. Peel the cucumbers, and cut them into wedges (see illus.).
3. Seed the green peppers, and cut them into ½-inch squares.
4. Cut the leek into ½-inch lengths, and peel and slice the ginger into thin ½-inch squares.
4. Combine all of the sauce ingredients in a small bowl.

FRYING
1. Heat a pan, oil its bottom and sides well, and return the excess oil to its container. Pour in three cups of fresh oil, and heat it to a moderate temperature (approximately 285 degrees F.). Lightly fry the cucumbers and chicken till they are thoroughly coated with oil. Remove them and drain. Just before removing these two ingredients, add the green peppers and lightly fry them till they begin to change color.
2. In the same pan, heat 1 tbsp oil. Sauté the red pepper been paste ginger, and leek at a low heat, and add the ingredients fried in the preceding step. After raising the heat to high, add all the sauce ingredients, and cook until the mixture thickens and becomes glossy. Add one tbsp oil from the sides of the pan. Serve immediately.

Cubed Chicken with Cashews and Bamboo Shoots

INGREDIENTS
7 oz chicken thighs
5 small bamboo shoots

3 oz cashew nuts
1 green pepper
small amount ginger root
½ leek

Seasonings

(for chicken)

¼ tsp salt
1 tsp soy sauce
dash monosodium glutamate
1 tbsp sake
dash pepper
dash baking powder
½ egg white
1½ tbsp cornstarch
small amount oil

Sauce

1 tsp sugar
1½ tbsp soy sauce
1 tbsp oil
1 tsp vinegar
dash monosodium glutamate
1 tbsp cornstarch and water mixture
1½ tbsp water

PREPARATIONS

1. After removing the tendons and cutting the chicken meat into ½-inch cubes, marinate it in a small bowl with the salt, soy sauce monosodium glutamate, sake, pepper, baking powder, egg white, cornstarch, and oil.

2. Clean the bamboo shoots, and cut them into wedges approximately the same size as the chicken cubes.

3. Seed the green peppers, and cut them into ½-inch squares.

4. Peel the ginger root, and cut it into thin ½-inch squares. Cut the leek into ½-inch lengths.

COOKING

1. Pour two cups of oil into a preheated pan. After the bottom and sides are thoroughly

coated, return the oil to its container. Pour in three or four cups of fresh oil; heat to a moderate temperature, and lightly fry the chicken, bamboo shoots, and green peppers. Remove and drain.

2. Dip the cashews into the moderately hot oil, remove, and drain.

3. Into the same pan, heat one tbsp oil, and sauté the leek and ginger. Add the fried chicken, vegetables, nuts, and all of the sauce ingredients. Cook over a high heat until the sauce thickens. Serve immediately.

Sautéed Chicken with Celery
(See page 38.)

INGREDIENTS

6 oz chicken thighs
4 oz celery
3 oz bamboo shoots
½ leek
small amount ginger root
1 egg
1 tbsp red pepper bean paste

Seasonings

(for chicken)

¼ tsp salt
1 tbsp sake
¼ tsp monosodium glutamate
dash pepper
dash baking powder
1 small egg
1 heaping tbsp cornstarch
1 tbsp oil

Sauce

½ tbsp soy sauce
1 tbsp sake
1½ tbsp vinegar
1 tsp sugar
1 tsp monosodium glutamate
1 tbsp cornstarch and water mixture
3 tbsp soup stock or water

PREPARATIONS

1. Remove bones and tendons from chicken, and cut it into julienne strips.

2. Julienne cut the celery and bamboo shoots slightly smaller than the chicken.

3. Cut the leek into ½-inch lengths and the ginger into thin ½-inch squares.

3. Mix together in a bowl the chicken, salt, sake, monosodium glutamate, pepper, baking powder, and egg, mix well. Add the corn-

starch and oil, and mix again.

4. Combine all the sauce ingredients.

COOKING

1. Heat a pan, oil it with one or two cups of oil, return the oil to the container. Pour in three cups of fresh oil, and heat it to a moderate temperature. Fry the chicken, bamboo shoots, and celery as you gradually increase the temperature of the oil. When the chicken has changed color, remove it and drain.

2. In the same pan, heat one tbsp oil, add the ginger, and lightly sauté it. Add the other vegetables, the chicken, and the sauce ingredients. When the sauce has thickened and become glossy, add one tbsp of oil around the side of the pan, and serve immediately.

Sautéed Chicken with Peanuts
(See page 55.)

INGREDIENTS
　　6 oz chicken thighs
　　3 oz peanuts
　　3 red peppers
　　15 grains Japanese pepper
　　½ leek
　　small amount ginger root
　　1 egg
　　Seasonings
　　(for chicken)
　　½ egg
　　¼ tsp salt
　　1 tbsp sake
　　¼ tsp monosodium glutamate
　　½ tsp soy sauce
　　dash baking powder
　　dash pepper
　　1½ tbsp cornstarch

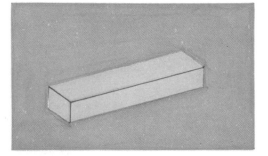

1 tbsp oil
Sauce
1½ tbsp soy sauce
1 tbsp vinegar
1 tbsp sugar
1 tbsp sake
½ tsp monosodium glutamate
1 tbsp cornstarch and water mixture
2 tbsp soup stock or water

PREPARATIONS

1. Cut the chicken into one-inch cubes.
2. Cut the red peppers into ½-inch lengths.
3. Cut the onions into ½-inch lengths.
4. Cut the ginger root into thin ½-inch squares.
5. Mix the chicken and the egg, salt, sake, soy sauce, monosodium glutamate, baking powder, pepper, cornstarch, and oil in a bowl.
6. Combine all the sauce ingredients in another bowl.

COOKING

1. Heat and oil a pan. Return the oil to its container. Pour in five tbsp of fresh oil, and over a moderate heat slowly sauté the red pepper and Japanese pepper until they turn black and their aroma and flavor have been transferred to the oil. Remove the pepper and discard. Next sauté the chicken in this oil.
2. When the chicken has changed color, add the leek and ginger first and then the sauce ingredients. When the sauce is thick and glossy, add the peanuts and one tbsp of oil from the side of the pan. Serve immediately.

Braised Chestnuts and Chicken

INGREDIENTS
½ young chicken (about 14 oz)
½ medium bamboo shoot
3 forest mushrooms
11 oz chestnuts
½ leek
small amount ginger root
2 garlic cloves
Seasonings
(for chicken)
small amounts of the following

sake
salt
soy sauce
monosodium glutamate
Sauce
6 or 7 cups soup stock
2 tbsp sake
½ tsp salt
½ tsp pepper
1 tbsp sugar
1 tbsp oyster sauce or Worcestershire sauce
2 tbsp soy sauce
1 tsp monosodium glutamate
2 tbsp cornstarch and water mixture
2 tbsp oil

PREPARATIONS

1. Without removing the bones, cut the chicken into convenient pieces.
2. Peel the chestnuts, and cut them in half.
3. If the mushrooms are dried, soak them in warm water. Remove their stalks, and julienne cut both them and the bamboo shoots.
4. Dice together the leek, ginger, and garlic.
5. Combine the chicken, salt, soy sauce, sake, and monosodium glutamate in a bowl.

COOKING

1. Heat two cups of oil in a pan. Dip the chestnuts in the oil, remove, and drain.
2. Raise the oil temperature to about 390 degrees F., and sauté the chicken. Remove and drain.
3. Heat two tbsp oil in the same pan, add sugar, and stir well. When the oil has boiled and the sugar has turned the color of caramel, add soup, chicken, and all other ingredients. Lower the heat, and cook briefly. Add sake, salt, pepper, sugar; cover,

and continue cooking. Finally add the oyster sauce, monosodium glutamate, cornstarch and water, and cook till thick. Add one tbsp of oil from the side of the pan. Serve immediately.

Breaded Chicken Breasts with Chestnuts (See page 27.)

INGREDIENTS
    5 boned chicken breasts
    4 oz chestnuts
    bread crumbs (fresh or prepared)
    2 egg yolks
Seasonings
    small amounts of the following
    salt
    pepper
    sake
    monosodium glutamate
    cornstarch

PREPARATIONS
1. Open the breasts and pound them lightly with the back of a butcher knife until they are of an even thickness and crisscrossed with fine indentations (see illus.).
   Sprinkle on seasonings, and roll the chicken in cornstarch.
2. Peel and chop the chestnuts fine and mix with the bread crumbs.
3. Beat the egg yolks in a small bowl.

COOKING
1. Dip the breasts in the egg yolks, coat them with chestnuts and bread crumbs, and fry till golden brown in oil heated to about 248 degrees F.

Duck Livers and Vegetable Sauté

INGREDIENTS
    1 stalk celery
    1 cucumber
    4 oz duck livers or chicken livers
Seasonings
(for livers)
    ¼ salt
    dash monosodium glutamate
    1 tbsp sake
    dash pepper
    dash baking powder
    ½ egg white
    1 heaping tbsp cornstarch
Sauce
    1 tbsp sake
    1 tbsp vinegar
    1 tbsp soy sauce
    1 tsp sugar
    1 tbsp cornstarch and water mixture
    small amounts chopped garlic, leek, and ginger
      root

PREPARATIONS
1. Thoroughly wash the celery, and dice it into 1-inch cubes; chop the celery leaves as well. Similarly dice the cucumber.
2. Clean the livers thoroughly, and dice them in to cubes of about ½ inch.
3. Combine the seasonings and the livers in a bowl, add the cornstarch, and mix well.
4. Combine the sauce ingredients in a bowl, add the diced leek, garlic, and ginger; finally stir in the cornstarch and water mix.

COOKING
1. Heat and oil a pan. Return the oil to the container. Pour in three cups of fresh oil, and heat it to about 180 degrees F. Lightly fry the livers, and add the celery and cucumber for a few moments. If the oil is too hot, the liver will form balls; if it is too cool the coating will peel off. Remove and drain.
2. In the same pan, heat three tbsp oil over a high flame. Add the sauce and all other ingredients. Cook until the sauce thickens. Add one tbsp of oil from the side of the pan, and serve.

Beef Dishes

Beef Sautéed with Vegetables

INGREDIENTS
7 oz lean beef
3 oz snow peas (or bamboo shoots, celery, or green peas)
½ leek
small amount ginger root

Seasonings
(for beef)
¼ tsp salt
1 tsp soy sauce
1 tsp sake
dash monosodium glutamate
1 tbsp water
dash pepper
dash baking powder
½ egg white
2 tbsp cornstarch

Sauce
1 tbsp oyster sauce
1 tbsp soy sauce
1 tbsp sake
1 tbsp sugar
½ tsp monosodium glutamate
1½ tbsp cornstarch and water mixture

PREPARATIONS
1.　Cut the beef into thin slices and then into bite-size pieces.　String the snow peas.
2.　Cut the leek into ½-inch lengths and the ginger root into thin ½-inch squares.
3.　Marinate the beef in the salt, soy sauce, sake, monosodium glutamate, water, pepper, baking powder, egg white, and cornstarch.

COOKING
1.　Heat and oil a pan; return the oil to its container.　Pour in three cups of fresh oil, heat to 245–250 degrees F., and lightly fry the beef.　When the beef rises to the surface of the oil, remove and drain it.
2.　Briefly fry, then remove and drain the snow peas.
3.　Heat one tbsp of oil in the same pan; add the leek and ginger, and sauté. Add the beef, snow peas, and sauce ingredients. Cook until the sauce thickens, and add one tbsp of oil from the side of the pan.

Seed Fried Beef

INGREDIENTS
4 oz beef loin
1 cup sesame seeds
½ egg

Seasonings
(for beef)
1 tsp soy sauce
dash salt
1 tbsp sake
1 tsp sugar
dash pepper
½ tsp monosodium glutamate
1 tbsp cornstarch

PREPARATIONS
1.　Slice the beef in slices ½ inch thick.
2.　Combine the soy sauce, salt, sake, pepper, sugar, monosodium glutamate, and the cornstarch in a bowl.　Add the beef, and marinate.
3.　Beat the egg.
4.　Pour seeds in a flat dish.
5.　Dip the slices of beef, one by one, into the egg and then into the seeds till they are thoroughly coated.

FRYING
1.　Heat about three cups of oil to from 300 to 320 degrees F.　Fry the slices of beef, one by one, in the oil, which must be at the

recommended temperatures to prevent the meat from sinking to the bottom of the pan.
2. When the seeds change color, the meat is done. Serve immediately.

Beef Fried in Waxed Paper

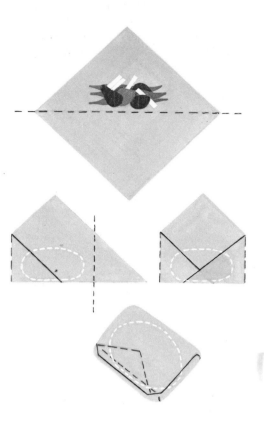

INGREDIENTS

4 oz beef loin
¾ leek
small amount ginger root
12 thin slices bamboo shoots (celery, or mushrooms, if bamboo shoot is unavailable)
waxed paper

Seasonings

(for beef)

1 tsp soy sauce
1 tbsp sake
1 tbsp oyster sauce
1 tsp sugar
dash pepper
½ tsp monosodium glutamate
1 tbsp cornstarch and water mixture
2 tbsp sesame oil

PREPARATIONS

1. Cut the beef into about 24 bite-size pieces.
2. Cut the leek into one-inch lengths, and julienne slice. Slice the ginger into slices ½ inch thick.
3. Wash and thin slice the bamboo shoots; drain.
4. Cut twelve sheets of waxed paper of equal sizes.
5. Into a bowl, put the beef, leek, ginger, soy sauce, sake, oyster sauce, sugar, pepper, and monosodium glutamate. Mix well. Add the cornstarch and water and the sesame oil. Mix again.
6. Place one slice of bamboo shoot in the middle of each piece of waxed paper, and top it with the marinated beef. Wrap as shown in the illustration. The sesame oil both flavors and prevents the food from adhering to the paper. If it is unavailable, plain salad oil, though less flavorsome, will serve the latter purpose.

FRYING

1. Heat about three cups of oil to from 340 to 355 degrees F. Place the wrapped beef, with the single layer of paper down, on a metal rack, and dip it into the hot oil. The oil should cover the meat packages. Move the rack lightly to promote even

cooking. When the meat changes color and the waxed paper turns light brown and crisp, remove from the pan, drain, and serve.

Sautéed Beef and Green Peppers

INGREDIENTS

6 oz beef loin
3 green peppers
½ bamboo shoot
½ leek

Seasonings
(for beef)
½ tsp salt
1 tbsp sake
½ tsp monosodium glutamate
dash baking powder
1 egg white
1 tbsp cornstarch

Sauce
1 tbsp soy sauce
1 tsp sugar
2 tsp sake
dash monosodium glutamate
2 tsp cornstarch and water mixture
1½ tbsp soup stock or water

PREPARATIONS

1. Julienne slice the beef with the grain. Combine it with the salt, sake, monosodium glutamate, baking powder, egg white, and the cornstarch.
2. Seed, wash, and julienne cut the green peppers.
3. Wash and thin slice the bamboo shoots; then julienne cut them.
4. Dice the leek fine.

SAUTÉEING

1. Heat the frying pan; oil it well, and return the oil to its container.
2. Pour three cups of fresh oil into the pan, and heat it to from 285 to 300 degrees F.
3. Sauté the beef and bamboo shoots, turning them constantly to prevent sticking to the pan.
4. When the beef changes color, remove it and the bamboo shoots; drain.
5. In the same pan, heat 2 tbsp oil over a high flame. Sauté the chopped leek and the green peppers. Add the beef and bamboo shoots. Stir in the sauce ingredients, and

cook till thick. Serve immediately.

This dish is an excellent accompaniment for sake or beer, but it serves equally well as a main course. Be especially carefully to avoid overcooking.

Vegetables Dishes

Chicken Breasts and Turbos

INGREDIENTS

2 oz boned chicken breast
½ can shelled turbos
small amounts spinach or Chinese cabbage

Seasonings

(for chicken)

½ tsp salt
½ tsp monosodium glutamate
1 tbsp cornstarch
1 egg white
3 tbsp water

(for spinach)

small amounts the following
salt
sake
monosodium glutamate
soup stock

(for turbos)

2 tbsp soup stock
1 tsp soy sauce
dash sake
dash sugar
dash monosodium glutamate
1 tbsp cornstarch and water mixture
small amount chicken fat

PREPARATIONS

1. Using the back of a butcher knife, pound the chicken to a fine pulp.
2. Boil the spinach very briefly, and squeeze the moisture from it.
3. To the chicken pulp, add three tbsp water; mix well. Season with the salt, monosodium glutamate, cornstarch, and add the egg white. Mix again.
4. Roll the stalk section of the spinach bunches in cornstarch. Holding the leaves in your hand, dip the stalks into the chicken mixture.

COOKING

1. Heat three cups of water to the boiling point. Turn the flame off. Dip the coated spinach stalks into the hot water till they have warmed thoroughly. Rinse carefully and put them into a bowl with the sake, salt, monosodium glutamate, and soup stock. Place in a steamer, and steam for about ten minutes. Remove to a serving plate.
2. Slice the turbos thin. Put them into a saucepan containing two tbsp of soup stock; add soy sauce, sugar, sake, monosodium glutamate, and heat. Add the cornstarch and water mixture, and heat till thick. Finally add the chicken fat, which will form small golden balls on the surface of the shellfish. Arrange the turbos among the coated spinach leaves on a serving plate.

Crab Roe and Chinese Cabbage
(See page 55.)

INGREDIENTS

1 lb Chinese cabbage
2 oz shelled crab meat
1 carrot
1 oz preserved or fresh crab roe

Seasonings

(for Chinese cabbage)

3 tbsp oil
2 cups soup stock
½ tsp salt
1 tbsp sake
dash pepper
dash monosodium glutamate
2½ tbsp cornstarch and water mixture
2 tbsp chicken fat

PREPARATIONS

1. Trim the cabbage into pleasing shapes by

removing the hard parts at the base and the unsightly ends of the leaves.

2. Cut them vertically into thin strips.

3. Grate the carrot and the preserved crab roe. If you use fresh crab roe, steam it beforehand; then cut it into fine pieces.

COOKING

In about three tbsp of hot oil, sauté the carrot and preserved crab roe. Add the crab meat, soup stock, Chinese cabbage, salt, sake, and pepper. Cover and cook over a low heat. When the Chinese cabbage is done, raise the heat, add the monosodium glutamate and cornstarch and water mixture. Cook until thick. Finally, add the chicken fat, and serve immediately.

Chinese Cabbage Rolls

INGREDIENTS

3 oz boned chicken breasts
3 oz pork fat
4 Chinese cabbage leaves
3 sheets dried seaweed

Seasonings
(for chicken)
small amounts of the following
salt
monosodium glutamate
sake

Sauce
½ tsp salt
1 tbsp sake
dash monosodium glutamate
dash pepper
1 tbsp cornstarch and water mixture
1 tbsp chicken fat
1 cup soup stock

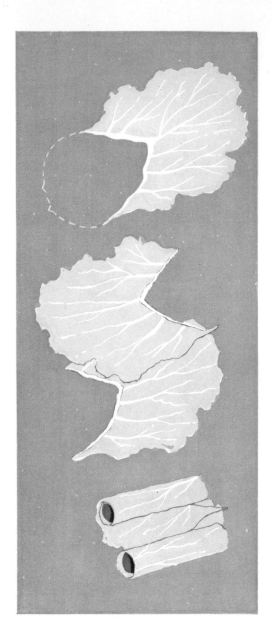

PREPARATIONS

1. Run the chicken and pork fat together through a meat grinder three times. If you do not have a meat grinder, chop the two together very fine.

2. Cut off the hard core of the cabbage leaves, boil them briefly, lay them flat, and cover with a dry cloth.

3. Coat the upper surface of the cabbage leaves with cornstarch, spread the seaweed on them, and thinly coat them with the ground chicken and pork fat.

4. Roll both ends toward the center (see

illus.), and place them on an oiled dish.

STEAMING
1. Place the cabbage rolls in a steamer, and cook for fifteen minutes.
2. Cut them into convenient pieces and arrange them, cut ends up, on a separate serving plate.
3. Mix the sauce ingredients, cook until thick, and serve over the cabbage rolls.

Variety Dish with Wheat Cakes

INGREDIENTS
2 oz boiled chicken
1 oz sliced ham
2 oz softened jellyfish
1 oz pork stomach
1 oz pork liver
1 cucumber
1 carrot
1 stalk celery
2¼ oz softened Chinese vermicelli
1 oz bean sprouts
10 fried wheat cakes (see below)
Sauce
2½ tbsp soy sauce
1½ tbsp vinegar
1 tsp monosodium glutamate
1 tbsp sesame oil
¾ tbsp prepared mustard

PREPARATIONS
1. Julienne cut all ingredients. Boil and chill the stomach and liver before cutting.
2. Combine all the sauce ingredients.
3. Combine all the cut ingredients and the sauce in a bowl; mix well.
4. This variety dish may be eaten alone, but it is more delicious accompanied by thin wheat cakes of flour and water well kneaded, rolled thin, and fried on both sides with no oil. Just before serving, steam the cakes, and serve them hot.

Eggplant Szechwan Sauté

INGREDIENTS
14 oz eggplant
4 oz ground pork
½ leek
½ oz garlic clove
small amount ginger root
Sauce
¼ tsp red pepper bean paste
1 cup soup stock
2 tbsp soy sauce
1 tbsp sake
1 tsp monosodium glutamate
2 heaping tsp sugar
1 tbsp cornstarch and water mixture
½ tsp vinegar
small amount oil

PREPARATIONS
1. Thinly slice the eggplants, and wash them in water.
2. Dice the leek, ginger root, and garlic, and place the leek in a separate dish.

SAUTÉEING
1. Fry the eggplant briefly in hot oil. Remove and drain.
2. Next sauté the pork. Add the garlic, ginger root, and soup stock. Add the eggplant, soy sauce, sake, monosodium glutamate, sugar, and braise for two or three minutes. Add the chopped leek and the cornstarch and water mixture, and finally the vinegar and oil. Serve hot.

Noodles and Rice

Steamed Meat Dumplings

INGREDIENTS

4 oz ground pork
1 bamboo shoot
1¾ oz softened dried forest mushroom
½ leek
Pastry
1⅓ cups flour
¾ cup hot water
small amount shortening (use sesame seed oil
   if desired)
Seasonings
½ tbsp sweetened bean paste
1 tbsp soy sauce
dash pepper
dash monosodium glutamate

PREPARATIONS

1. Dice the bamboo shoot, mushroom, and leek.
2. Sift the flour into a bowl, and mixing constantly, slowly add the hot water. Add the shortening, and mix well. Knead on a floured board to make a firm dough.
3. Form the dough into a cylinder, and cut it into fifteen equal round slices.
4. Working from the center outward, roll each slice into a thin patty.

MAKING THE DUMPLINGS

1. Briefly sauté the pork in 1 tbsp hot oil. To it add the bean paste, soy sauce, pepper, and monosodium glutamate. Add the bamboo shoots and forest mushrooms and, finally, the leek. Sauté lightly.

2. Slightly lower than the center line of each pastry patty, place a small amount of the sautéed meat filling. Fold the patty in half, and press the edges together firmly making small pleats in the surface (see illus.). Do not use too much flour as it prevents the layers of dough from adhering to each other.
3. Arrange the dumplings on a plate coated with sesame seed oil, and steam them for from eight to ten minutes.

These dumplings, though made of the same dough and filling, taste different according to the way they are cooked: fried, steamed, or heated with soup.

TO FRY   Oil the bottom of a frying pan. Arrange the dumplings, flat side down, in the pan, cover, and cook over a medium heat till the bottoms are golden brown. Pour in ⅓ cup of water, cover, and continue cooking till all of the moisture has evaporated.

WITH SOUP Steam the dumplings first; then serve them in bowls of hot soup flavored with salt or soy sauce to taste.

NOTE: in the latter case, pay closer attention to closing the edges tightly, and worry less about making attractive pleats in the surface of the dough.

Thin-skin Meat Dumplings

INGREDIENTS

2 oz lean pork
2 oz pork fat
2 oz spinach
2 oz fortified flour
small amount cornstarch for rolling pastry
2 oz uncooked glutinous rice (or plain rice)
Seasonings
¼ tsp salt
dash pepper
dash monosodium glutamate
few drops sesame oil
2 tsp sake

PREPARATIONS

1. Mix the water and flour into a stiff dough.

2. Shape the dough into sixteen small balls, roll them in cornstarch, and press them into patties about three inches in diameter. Lay three or four on top of each other, and roll as thin as possible. The cornstarch will prevent them from sticking together.

3. Wash the rice, add just enough water to cover it, and cook it for about twenty minutes.

4. Boil the pork fat for twenty minutes; cool, and chop fine.

5. Briefly boil the spinach—it must not lose its bright green color—squeeze the moisture from it, and chop.

6. Grind the lean pork, and combine it with the rice, pork fat, and spinach. Season with salt, pepper, monosodium glutamate, and sesame oil.

7. Place filling in the center of each thin skin, and bring the pastry to the top on all sides. The dumplings are more attractive topped which diced ham.

8. Oil the bottom of a steamer, place the dumplings in it, and steam them for from two to three minutes. Before they are done, sprinkle water on the parts of the pastry covered with cornstarch to make them transparent.

Crab Fried Rice

INGREDIENTS

    3 oz canned crab
    1 oz canned green peas (garnish)
    2 eggs
    1 leek
    2 cups cold boiled rice

Seasonings
3 tbsp oil
¾ tsp salt
dash monosodium glutamate

PREPARATIONS

1. Remove all bone from the canned crab.

2. Finely chop the leek.

3. The rice should be cooked harder than usual and must be thoroughly cold.

FRYING

1. Heat a frying pan; oil it with two or three cups of oil. Return the oil to its container.

2. Add three tbsp fresh oil to the pan, heat it, and add two well beaten eggs. Stirring constantly, add the cold rice, and sauté briefly. Add the crab meat, and mix with a cutting motion of a spatula. Season with salt and monosodium glutamate, and garnish with green peas.

   In stirring, be sure to break up all lumps of cooked rice. Chopped cooken meats, ham, sausage, or shrimp may be substituted for canned crab.

Spicy Szechwan Noodles with Chicken

INGREDIENTS

    5 oz chicken thigh with bone
    ½ cucumber
    2 oz softened jellyfish
    9 oz Chinese noodles
    Sauce
    7 tbsp soy sauce
    1 tbsp vinegar
    1 tsp monosodium glutamate
    2 heaping tbsp sugar

3 tbsp tabasco
small amount pepper oil
1 leek
small amount ginger root
1½ tbsp sesame seed oil

PREPARATIONS

1. Bring the chicken and water rapidly to a boil. Lower the flame and boil for from ten to fifteen minutes. Remove the chicken. Set the broth aside. Take out the thigh bone, and cut the meat in thin strips.
2. Thin slice the cucumber. The already softened jellyfish should be soaked in cold water for another two hours and then drained.

COOKING

1. Boil the noodles in plenty of water till they are done, but slightly hard. Drain well, and cool. Do not use water to chill, however, since this greatly reduces the flavor of the noodles. If you are cooking large quantities of noodles, spread them on large plates and direct an electric fan over them. Pour 1½ tbsp sesame seed oil over the noodles and mix well to both increase their flavor and prevent them from sticking together.
2. Divide the noodles into servings and garnish with cucumber, jellyfish, and sliced chicken.
3. Combine all the sauce ingredients, and pour over the noodles.
NOTE: Blend the sauce ingredients only after adding the tabasco, pepper oil, leek, and ginger.

Fried Noodles and Thin Sliced Pork
(See page 55.)

INGREDIENTS
9 oz Chinese noodles

3 oz pork loin
3 oz canned bamboo shoots
2 dried forest mushrooms
small amount spinach
Seasonings
(for the pork)
dash salt
dash sake
dash pepper
1 tbsp cornstarch and water mixture
small amount oil
Sauce
2 cups soup stock
2 tbsp soy sauce
1 tbsp sake
1 tsp monosodium glutamate
dash pepper
dash salt

PREPARATIONS

1. Slice the pork, bamboo shoots, and softened forest mushrooms thin.
2. Wash and drain the spinach.
3. Marinate the pork in the salt, sake, pepper, cornstarch and water, and small amount of oil.
4. Bring about six cups of water to a boil, put the noodles into it, and stirring to prevent their sticking together, cook them till approximately half done. Chill in cold running water and drain well. Sprinkle a few drops of soy sauce on them and mix well.

FRYING

1. Heat the frying pan, pour in one cup of oil, coat the sides and bottom well, and add the noodles. Constantly moving the pan to prevent burning, fry the noodles on both sides till they are lightly browned. Drain and remove to a serving dish.
3. In the same pan, fry the pork, mushrooms, and bamboo shoots in one cup of hot oil. Drain.
4. Add two cups of soup stock, soy sauce, sake, monosodium glutamate, salt and pepper to the same pan. After bringing it to a boil, add the pork, bamboo shoots, and mushrooms. Season to taste, and add the spinach. Finally thicken with the cornstarch and water mixture.

Pour over the fried noodles and serve immediately.

Spring Rolls

INGREDIENTS

Shells
1 cup flour
dash salt
small amount oil

Filling
3 oz pork loin
5 oz cabbage
2 forest mushrooms
4 oz bamboo shoots
1 green pepper

Seasonings
3 tbsp soy sauce
1 tsp sugar
1 tsp salt
3 tbsp sake
dash pepper
dash monosodium glutamate
2 tbsp cornstarch and water mixture
3 tbsp soup stock

PREPARATIONS

Shells

To the mixture of salt and one cup of flour, gradually add enough water to make a stiff dough. Knead well, chill in the refrigerator, and knead again. Divide the dough into ten equal parts, and roll each into a very thin patty.

Heat a frying pan, coat it lightly with a small amount of oil, and wipe off excess oil with a paper towel. Fry each patty till the edges are dry. Set aside till needed.

Filling

1. Julienne cut the pork; sprinkle it with salt, a few drops of sake, and cornstarch. Set aside.
2. Julienne cut the green peppers, cabbage, bamboo shoots, and mushrooms.

3. Fry pork, bamboo shoots, and mushrooms lightly in hot oil. Remove and drain.
4. Dip the vegetables into the same hot oil, and remove immediately.
5. Heat the same frying pan, oil it, return the oil to its container, and add four tbsp fresh oil. Add all the meat and vegetables as well as the seasonings and sauté quickly. When the sauce is thick, add a small amount of sesame seed oil from the side of the pan. Remove and chill.

Making the Rolls

1. Following the steps shown in the illustration, put suitable amounts of filling on each pre-fried patty, and roll. Seal them with a paste made of flour and water. Heat oil for frying to about 175-210 degrees F. Fry one roll at a time, beginning with a low flame and gradually raising it so that the inside of the roll will be done and the outside crisp, but not burned.

Pay close attention to the following points.
1. Spread the filling evenly on the patty.
2. Do not tear the patty in rolling.
3. The oil must be neither too hot nor too cool.
4. The fried outer shells must be crisp and tender.

Shrimp or shell fish may be substituted for pork.

Desserts

Steamed Fruit Pudding

INGREDIENTS

- 2 oz raisins
- 1 oz orange peel
- 1 oz drained canned cherries
- 1 oz angelica
- 3 eggs
- 5 oz pork fat
- 3 tbsp flour

Seasonings

(for fruit)

- ½ cup water
- 1 tbsp sugar
- 2 tbsp oil
- small amount lard or other shortening

(for cake)

- 3 tbsp sugar
- 1½ tsp baking powder

(for syrup)

- 4 tbsp sugar
- 1 tsp cornstarch
- 6 tbsp water

PREPARATIONS

1. Wash the raisins in hot water and chop fine.
2. Cut the pork fat into slices ⅛ inch thick.
3. Chop the cherries, orange peel, and angelica.
4. In a saucepan combine ¼ cup water, the chopped raisins, 1 tbsp sugar, 2 tbsp oil, and cook briefly.
5. Grease and line an oven-proof bowl with the slices of pork fat (see illus.). Add the raisin mixture and then the other chopped fruits to make layers (see illus.).
6. In a separate bowl, lightly beat three egg yolks. In still another container, beat three egg whites till stiff.
7. In a medium mixing bowl, combine 3 tbsp flour, egg whites and yolks, 3 tbsp sugar, and 1½ tsp baking powder; mix well.

STEAMING

1. Pour the batter on top of the fruit, place the container in a steamer, and steam for about thirty minutes. Remove, invert on a serving plate, peel off the pork fat, and set

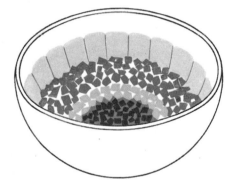

aside.

2. Prepare the syrup by bringing to a boil 6 tbsp of water and 4 tbsp of sugar and then adding 1 tsp cornstarch. Cook till thick and clear.

3. Pour this syrup over the pudding just before serving.

Sweet Fruits

INGREDIENTS

    5 arrowhead bulbs
    1 tbsp raisins
    2 tbsp crystallized plums
    1 tbsp crystallized melons
    2 heaping tbsp cornstarch
    5 egg yolks

PREPARATIONS

1. Peel the arrowhead bulbs, and cut them into small, thin squares.

2. Cut the plums and melons into similar squares.

3. Mix the cornstarch with five egg yolks, add 1 cup of water, and mixing constantly, bring to a boil.

4. Add the arrowhead and other fruits to this mixture.

COOKING

1. Pour ½ cup oil into a frying pan. Add all the above ingredients, and taking care that they do not scorch, sauté them well. After adding one cup of sugar, continue sautéeing briefly. When all the fruits are thoroughly heated, add one tbsp oil from the side of the pan. When the oil has risen to the top of the mixture, serve.

This light dish of fruits and sugar sauce is a fine dessert or a pleasant dish to be served between main courses. The natural flavors for the fruits are the main attraction.

Chinese Candied Sweet Potatoes

INGREDIENTS

    14 oz sweet potatoes
    1 cup sugar
    small amount sesame seeds
    3 tbsp water
    small amount sesame seed oil

PREPARATIONS

1. Peel the potatoes, and cut them into bite-size pieces.

2. Coat a plate with sesame seed oil.

COOKING

1. Heat 5 cups of oil to 250 degrees F. Turning them constantly, fry the potatoes in this oil over a moderate flame. Just before removing them, turn the flame high and brown the potatoes.

2. Into the same pan, heat three tbsp water and one cup sugar. Cook until the mixture thickens and is a golden color.

3. Add the sesame seeds, and then the sweet potatoes. Stirring constantly, cook until the potatoes are thoroughly coated with the sugar syrup. Remove to the previously oiled plate.

4. Serve while hot, but provide each guest with a small bowl of cold water in which to dip his potato before eating. This both lowers the temperature to a more comfortable range and hardens the sugar coating to the consistency of brittle candy.

Light Custard and Fruits in Syrup

INGREDIENTS
  10 strips agar-agar gelatin
  2 tsp sugar
  2 tbsp almond powder
  2 tbsp canned milk
  3 cups water

Syrup
  1¼ cups sugar
  2½ cups water
  fruits for garnish

PREPARATIONS
1. Wash the agar-agar, and boil it in three cups of water over a low heat for fifteen minutes or until the liquid has reduced to one-third its original quantity. Strain well and chill.
2. Combine the almond powder and sugar, and disolve it by gradually adding the canned milk. Add the liquid from the boiled agar-agar, pour the mixture into a mold, and chill till firm in the refrigerator.
3. Mix 1½ cups sugar and 3 cups water in a separate pan. Bring to a boil, and strain through a cloth. Chill well in the refrigerator.
4. Pour the chilled syrup into a serving bowl, garnish with canned fruits (fruit cocktail), and after removing the chilled custard from the mold and cutting it into small cubes, float it on top of the syrup. If the fruit sinks, increase the density of the syrup by adding more sugar.

   If prepared Chinese almond powder is unavailable for this tempting summer dessert, finely chopped blanched almonds or English walnuts may be used instead.

Fish Dishes

Batter Fried Fish

INGREDIENTS

6 oz fish fillet
3 egg whites
small amount chestnuts

Seasonings
(for the fish)
dash salt
dash monosodium glutamate
dash pepper
dash sake
1 tbsp cornstarch

Batter
4 tbsp flour
2 tbsp cornstarch
dash monosodium glutamate

PREPARATIONS

1. Cut the fish into strips about $2\frac{1}{2}$ inches long by $\frac{1}{2}$ inch wide.
2. Crush six or seven chestnuts to a powder.
3. Combine the salt, monosodium glutamate, pepper, and sake in a bowl. Add the fish; mix well. Sprinkle the cornstarch and ground chestnuts on the fish, and mix thoroughly.

Batter
1. Beat the egg whites till stiff.
2. Add monosodium glutamate, flour, and cornstarch. Mix well.

FRYING

1. Coat the fish with batter, and put them one by one into a pan of oil heated slightly. Gradually raise the temperature of the oil and pour the hot oil over the fish.

2. When the batter has begun to color slightly, remove and drain.
3. Serve with pepper or tomato catchup.

Braised Fish

INGREDIENTS

$1\frac{1}{2}$ lb white meat fish
1 tbsp chopped celery
$\frac{1}{2}$ leek
1 tbsp chopped ginger root
$\frac{1}{2}$ tbsp chopped garlic

Seasonings
1 tsp red pepper bean paste
2 cups soup stock
$1\frac{1}{2}$ tbsp soy sauce
2 tbsp sake
dash salt
dash pepper
1 tbsp sugar
1 tsp monosodium glutamate
4 tbsp oil
1 tsp vinegar

PREPARATIONS

1. Clean the fish, and make diagonal incisions on both sides.
2. Fry it in hot oil until brown.

Braising
1. Pour 2 tbsp oil into a pan, and lightly sauté the ginger, garlic, and pepper bean paste. Add two cups soup stock and the fried fish, plus soy sauce, sake, salt, monosodium glutamate, sugar, pepper. Cover and cook at a moderate heat for about 15 minutes. When nearly done, add the chopped celery and leek. Thicken with cornstarch and water, and turning the pan to prevent the fish from sticking to the bottom, add four tbsp oil and 1 tsp vinegar. Serve hot.

Fried Red Snapper with Sweet and Sour Sauce

INGREDIENTS

1 red snapper (about 14 oz)

1½ leek
1 tsp chopped ginger root
Seasonings
(for the fish)
1½ tsp salt
dash pepper
dash monosodium glutamate
dash sake
1 egg white
2½ tbsp cornstarch and water mixture
Sauce
8 tbsp sugar
8 tbsp vinegar
½ tsp salt
1 tbsp soy sauce
3 tbsp tomato catchup
2 tbsp cornstarch and water mixture
3 tbsp soup stock
small amounts chopped leek and ginger root

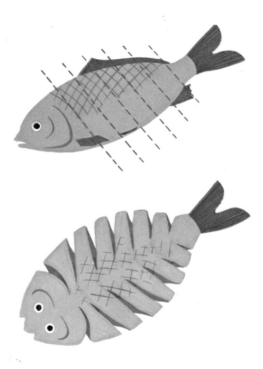

PREPARATIONS

1. Leaving the head and tail intact, clean the fish, and make six or seven incisions to the bone (see illus.) along both its sides.
2. Coat the inside and outside of the fish with a mixture of salt, pepper, monosodium glutamate, sake, egg white, and cornstarch, making sure that the coating reaches into the cuts along the sides. Sprinkle with a small amount of water.

FRYING

1. Gently slip the fish into three cups of oil heated to 355 degrees F., and fry until brown. (First holding the fish by its tail, dip it into the oil until the slits open as shown in the illustration and until the surface is crisp. Then gently lower it on its side into the oil, and fry for from fifteen to twenty minutes.)
2. Drain, and keep warm till needed.

SAUCE

1. Mix the sugar, vinegar, salt, soy sauce, tomato catchup, cornstarch and water mixture in a bowl.
2. Heat a pan, and pour in the mixed ingredients plus three tbsp of soup stock. Bring to a boil to thicken. Add the chopped leek, garlic, and ginger root, and finally four tbsp of oil. Pour the sauce over the fish, and serve immediately.

Crab Meat Puffs

INGREDIENTS
    2 oz canned crab meat
    2 oz bamboo shoots
    1 small piece ginger root
    1 leek
    5 egg whites
Seasonings
    dash salt
    3 tbsp milk
    1 heaping tbsp flour
    dash monosodium glutamate
    2 tbsp soup stock

PREPARATIONS
1.   Remove all of the bone from the crab meat.
2.   Chop the bamboo shoots and ginger root fine.
3.   Cut the leek into ½-inch sections.
4.   Beat the egg whites till stiff, and add the flour, milk, monosodium glutamate, and salt. Mix well.
5.   Combine this mixture with the crab meat and vegetables.

FRYING
1.   Heat a frying pan, add one cup of oil to coat the sides and bottom, return the oil to its container.
2.   Pour five tbsp fresh oil into the same pan. Drop the crab meat mixture by spoonfuls into the hot oil.   Turning them constantly to prevent sticking, fry till they are puffy and float to the surface of the oil.   Remove and drain well.

Crab Rolls

INGREDIENTS
    1 oz crab meat (canned)
    2 oz bamboo shoot
    1 oz dried forest mushroom
    4 oz cabbage
    1 green pepper
    2 eggs
Seasonings
    1 tbsp soy sauce
    1 tbsp sake
    1 tsp sugar
    1½ tsp monosodium glutamate
    dash pepper
    2 tbsp soup stock
    dash salt
    4 tbsp cornstarch and water mixture
    (for eggs)
    3 tbsp cornstarch and water mixture

PREPARATIONS
1.   Julienne slice the bamboo shoots, softened mushrooms, cabbage, and green pepper.
2.   Beat the eggs, and add 3 tbsp cornstarch and water.   Mix well.
3.   Heat a pan, and thinly coat it with oil.
4.   Fry the egg in a thin sheet.   Set aside till needed.   A small amount of egg should be left uncooked.
5.   Heat oil in a frying pan, and sauté all the vegetables plus the soy sauce, sake, sugar, monosodium glutamate, pepper, and soup stock.
6.   Spread the mixture on a plate, and top it with crab meat.
Chop the entire mixture fine.
7.   Prepare a paste for sealing the rolls by mixing the uncooked egg with a little cornstarch.

Soups

Oriental Radish and Pork Soup

INGREDIENTS
4 oz pork loin
14 oz oriental radish
small piece leek
small piece ginger root

Batter
1 egg
3 heaping tbsp cornstarch
1 tbsp water

Seasonings
1 tsp salt
1 tbsp sake
dash pepper
½ tsp monosodium glutamate
7½ cups water

PREPARATIONS
1.   Cube the pork (about ½-inch to a side),

FINAL COOKING
1.   Put the meat, radish, leek, and ginger into 7½ cups of water, and cook for forty minutes over a low flame.
2.   When the liquid has reduced by half, add the salt, sake, pepper, monosodium glutamate, and serve.

and peel and cut the radish into small diamond shapes.
2.   Mix the egg with one tbsp water and three heaping tbsp cornstarch to make a batter.
3.   Sprinkle monosodium glutamate, salt, and pepper on the meat, roll it in cornstarch, and dip it into the batter.
4.   Fry the meat in hot oil until it begins to brown.   Drain.

Sweet Corn Soup

INGREDIENTS
    1 can sweet corn
    2 eggs
    4 cups soup stock
    Seasonings
    1 tsp salt
    1 tbsp sake
    dash pepper
    1 tsp monosodium glutamate
    2 tbsp cornstarch and water mixture

PREPARATIONS
Heat the soup and corn, stirring frequently. Add salt, sake, pepper, and monosodium glutamate. Thicken with the cornstarch mixture, and turn off, or greatly lower, the heat. Beat the eggs, and stirring the liquid constantly, pour them in a thin stream into the hot soup. The soup must not be boiling when the thin stream of egg is added.

Stir immediately after adding the corn to prevent it from sinking to the bottom and burning.

Regulate the thickness of the soup to taste by varying the amount of cornstarch.

Three-flavor Soup

INGREDIENTS
    2 oz boned chicken breasts
    2 oz white meat fish fillet
    2 oz abalone
    1 oz bamboo shoots
    1 oz mushrooms
    small amount spinach
    ½ egg white
    4 cups soup stock

Seasonings
(for the chicken and fish)
dash salt
1 tbsp sake
dash pepper
dash monosodium glutamate
1 tbsp cornstarch
(for the soup)
1 tsp salt
1 tbsp sake
dash pepper
½ tsp monosodium glutamate

PREPARATIONS
1.   Cut the chicken, fish, and abalone into thin slices.
2.   Wash the spinach, and cut it into convenient pieces.
3.   Beat the egg in a bowl, add the salt, sake, pepper, monosodium glutamate, and cornstarch, and coat the fish and chicken carefully in this mixture.

COOKING
1.   To four cups of soup stock add the abalone, bamboo shoots, mushrooms, salt, sake, pepper, and monosodium glutamate, and bring the mixture to a boil. Add the chicken and fish, piece by piece. Skim off the froth that forms on the top, and season to taste. Add the spinach, and just before serving, sprinkle in a few drops of chicken fat.